Skull Kingdoms:
an Imaginary Omnibus

Matthew Burnside

For information contact:
Unsolicited Press
Portland, Oregon
www.unsolicitedpress.com
orders@unsolicitedpress.com
619-354-8005

Cover Design: Kathryn Gerhardt
Editor: Summer Stewart

ISBN: 978-1-963115-02-4

WITH GRATITUDE TO THE FOLLOWING VENUES

Postlunar Lovesong appeared in *Pithead Chapel*; Young Escher Reconsiders the Human Heart as a Series of Tessellations Unspooling Toward Eternity + All of Tomorrow's Rust is Electric appeared in *No Contact*; Three Prayers appeared in *Rejection Letters*; The Prognosticators appeared in *Okay Donkey*; Secondhand Heavens appeared in *Cartridge Lit*; Moments After My Wife Informs Me from the Passenger Seat that Lightning is Merely a Bundle a Negatively Charged Ions But What We Famously Know as Lightning is Actually Just the Positive Flash of Afterlight Crawling its Way Wounded Back Up the Sky, appeared in *The Hunger*; Salutis in Solitudine: A Game of Language & Loneliness was a finalist in *Art & Letter's Unclassifiables Contest*

This book is dedicated to all the childish games that saved us.

& to You, who has endured.

Keep Being.

You are not writing into a void.

You may, however, be writing into avoid.

I

ILL-BEGOTTEN GAMES

"If you think of this Nothingness as mere blankness, and you hold onto the idea of blankness, and kind of grisly about it, you haven't understood it. Nothingness is really like the nothingness of space, which contains the whole universe. All the sun, moon, and stars and the mountains, and rivers, and the good men, and the bad men, and the animals, and the insects, the whole bit. All are contained in Void. So out of this Void comes Everything and You Are It. What else could you be?"

—Alan Watts

AUTHOR'S NOTE: Read the pieces in accordance with the rules at the bottom of each page.

Postlunar Lovesong (Moontag*)

In dreams we drill a hole into Yes, just to un-itch a scratch. Play jump rope with power lines, skip water across stones to steal something that isn't sold to us in bright blue bottles. Fill our pockets with *If, Ever. Miss, Mist, Maybe,* a swim through sharper skies swinging elbows like butterfly knives just to feel something real, until our sinking is singing. Cut, touch. Every kill a kind of kiss. Building makeshift tongues to trill the future into something less fricative, something more glide: all the while sonorously screaming Every tree winking darkly, every blade of grass glaring. Wishing for rabbit holes to fall through us

---

* *Read dreamily, as if lost in a trance from which one may never return.

Young Escher Reconsiders the Human Heart as a Series of
Tessellations Unspooling Toward Eternity (Existential
Hopscotch*)

1. Baby Escher sits disentangling the beveled edges of his pet mirrors, caressing their convexities. Counts the reflections that slither slipshod through the apertures of his peripheral drift. "What pretty symmetries you have!" he says, gathering them all into a terrarium for playtime, where he will use a Möbius strip for a rattle, Penrose spiral as pacifier.

2. Teen Escher, sporting an isosceles mohawk, clicks his lighter at the parabolic silence inside a keyhole. Contemplates the tyranny of time's passage afforded through such a thin sliver's portal while squeezing swans through the eye of an accordion. Cancels his date to ponder the loneliness of every parallel line fated never to meet each other.

3. Old Escher gambols through the garden of his precious polyhedra, counting ivies stippled, dripping drunk with despair under a mollusk-pink cubist rainfall. Dreams of spheres, skulls, sunken cathedrals.

4. Dying Escher considers the too-many names of the numinous: Chameleons in outer space, shadows slowdancing inside crystals, the spectral howling laughter of a prism. Everything eventually chiseled into being by love's lithe lithographers, emblazoned like snowcrash. All the hands meant to hold. Every mouth made for singing. Infinity, at last, braided.

---

* Read while simultaneously tracing infinity symbols in the air, faster & faster, or over an ostensibly solid surface

All of Tomorrow's Rust is Electric (Hide-and-Seek*)

If in a dog's eye a universe you find, follow it. Some secondhand sun to pocket. Chase what may a warmblink brings that knows no harm. Starflung, as nighttail is to twitching. As harp is to ear, ripe is to rind. As sin is to singing. Or how lovely the longingly of rain's pretending, leaden even by some iniquity of clouds. Or, say, some fulsome feather swerving. Someone else's sky of grief that you drag home whole &, in your teeth's attics, furnish with formidable joy

---

* Read read to a dog or cat, stray or domesticated, makes no difference; it must receive a treat afterward for listening

Three Prayers

I. In Defiance, RE: The Brazen Fuckery of These Darkloom Days (Mother May I?*)

(DEAR WHOMEVER,
tired of mirrors slithering
tired of pasting faces tired
of every pitted pensive pendulum
above all tired of being tired
fed up from feeding
all these fanciful metaphors of what it means to be a
shadow electrified inside a stock body
this surly bond of knots, snagged or snarling
stumbling through the dark loom of whatever the
long lean nights even mean anymore
I mean what the fuck
Jesus?
what the fuck
Clocks?
what the fuck
Language?
Mother Tongue of Light:
sawdust, teeth, tonsil-
what words for hope don't dust away zephyr
red, windblown about in a wreckage? this finds

---

* Scream it at the top of one's lungs, if only internally

you
I hope
Well?)

II. Prayer Prayed by Skin of One's Teeth (Telephone*)

(DEAR LORD OF THIS GODDAMN EARTH! Forgive us all the diamonds we buried in our backyard yesterday in the vain hope that tomorrow might dig them up & call them pretty. Soft, trembling edgeless things but sharp enough still to lop the head off a scarecrow. Send word that the birds have abandoned us for brighter fields to haunt—[mumbling unintelligibly for quite some lines longer. Ad infinitum Et Cetera, but no more hallelujahs left to sing............... ....…..…])

---

* At the mumbling part, you must mumble a few lines of unique nonsense, all your own

III. The Snow That Once Was Made of Glass It Is Falling
   Now (Ring Around a Rosy*)

(DEAR WHATEVER made you feel so small was wrong & all the
things that could not possibly be poems now are.   So: *There*.)

---

* Find the nearest mirror. Write Yes on it. Mean it now, today, tomorrow,
forever

Watching That One Scene from It's a Wonderful Life Again,
Seven Minutes Until Midnight (Charades*)

That one where George considers jumping off the bridge into the icy water below / yeah, that's the one / always has been / on days like today as I stare into a hole in my house / this drafty old barn / ("we don't use money in Heaven"…*"well, it comes in real handy down here, bud!"*) / periodic reminder the only thing keeping me fastened to this earth some days / is the fear of failing a stranger I might otherwise accidentally save / through some indiscriminate yet ordinary act of kindness / a pharmacist in the throes of grief / big brother fallen through thinning ice / or rattled bank patrons / that can be enough, you know? / we all get scared sometimes / tired, too / so here I am speaking through the screen again / asking you to step back out of the snow / warm yourself beside the fire/ of that little one-room lighthouse / there is still some warmth to be had in this old world / in spite of its scurvy spiders / cynical little web spinners / I'll play the part of Clarence / we won't let them win / all the Mr. Potters of this world / I am asking you to recall / Zuzu's petals / all the loose & lovely bannisters

/ the hydrangea bushes of Mary's eyes / school dance swimming pools parted / & three most exciting sounds in the world—anchor chains, plane motors, & train whistles / I am asking you to imagine the moon, lassoed…the moonbeams tomorrow that shall shoot out of our fingers & toes & ends of our hair / saying "I want to live again. Please, God, let me live again" / reminding you there will always be another stranger / in need of saving / begging you to believe it / so I may believe it myself / that in the whole vast configuration of things / you are still a rich man

---

* Read as the reincarnation of Jimmy Stewart, Donna Reed, or Clarence the Angel

Hope Hurts (Musical Chairs*)

Otherwise it's not hope
All art begins with a broken heart Bit
of bad light, some good shadows
And the crow stuck on a cloud isn't caught in a loop
Isn't glitching—it just knows the secret of flight How
not to fight the wind of its own dreaming Give in or
let one's wings bend too far inward
Nor does it fear the papercuts of origami futures
(Its imminent collapse; *it was always going to collapse*
. . .) So much so that it stops folding itself forward
Fashioning a beak, rebuilding a makeshift body Some calamitous,
jangling vessel to sail it across These many
nights to come until it crashes. Explodes Into some
lovelier star.   Becomes a sky all its own

---

* Read only under aegis of natural starlight

Nameless #9 (Floor is Lava[*])

1. Fill every fissure, slit, slat, wound, aperture with quicksand
2. Pretend yourself a desert
3. Wait for rain that will never come
4. To rinse away the stain of what was never there

---

[*] Forget him/her/they, who is not worth the burning

There's a Secret Internet Inside Me Where Everyone is Happy (Bloody Knuckles*)

But most nights I still disappear inside my Nintendo. Feel its electric tongue tickling. Count clicks instead of sheep. There's a fear life is speed running me. I can tell by the humming & I am just as lost as you are. Fishhook in my heart & somewhere, still, a sea. This poem won't save you, but it may buy you some time to remember that the moon is not a piñata filled with blood, so why are you hitting it like that? Sunlight is not a tourniquet, nor a Christmas ornament to weigh down the branches of a nameless tree. Bees are not a bullseye; dreams are not darts. The human heart is not a shimmering radio. There's a fear the answer will remain elusive. That, try as you might, the story you wrote for the boy with an unexplained nose bleed on the curb, whose tissue was blossoming out like a paper rose, whom you saw exactly once & never again, will never be read, at least not by him. There's a void inside your belly button, there's a sailboat in your shin, & there's no way of knowing, though you will write many more stories only to return to the boy on the curb, red rose blooming out of his right nostril, a story you began exactly once but never finished, will never finish, for fear of how it may end

---

* You can still save someone

18

Nameless #13 (Thumb War*)

Whatever you do don't imagine a boy imagining tiny propellers on his
tongue—the lifting fizz, hanger pangs in his teeth like balloons bobbing
under love-starved bleachers, hungry for helium dreams

Whatever you do, forget the boy who craves secret labyrinths in his
bathtub since back before birth, practicing so tenderly, tracing outlines
of ghosts across the surface of the water—carving out their silhouettes
over sudsy, peach-thin skin

Whatever you do don't remind him when he speaks to you, says remind
me I'm alive to the bony wolf outside his window—"Take me clear
across the long lean night, heart strobing like a final boss at the end of
the last level. Make me saga: Something more than nothing. A story, a
something, an anything."

Whatever you do don't nod back when he nods, cross-stitched with
scars, entering the forbidden forest, his fryingpan feet sunk in mud. As
he disentombs the glitch in his chest, places it
somewhere it'll never be found again. Says, there is no undoing
the doneness of some things & with glowing
bandages buries it, some spherical moon made of glass. Rising, risen—
Punchdrunk pink with flight at last

---

* If a ghost haunts you, just haunt it back

*Moments After My Wife Informs Me From the Passenger Seat
That Lightning is Merely a Bundle of Negatively Charged Ions
But What We Famously Know as Lightning is Actually Just the
Positive Flash of Afterlight Crawling its Way Wounded Back
Up the Sky . . . (Jinx*)*

I question her about the soundness of science as she flicks a soda tab at
me. Then I tell her there's no shame in feeling things deeply but it is
occasionally a very tiring pastime. That I could carve my longing for
imaginary people into the shape of a chandelier, press such frangible
sorrows into the arms of all my hypothetical poems like so many
gathered petals, I would. Damn the clichés—so long as the cynical
wolves are circling we must risk the softness of lamplight, right? Then I
tell her about how often I worry myself mad for my former & future
students, their well-being, mental health & happiness. Spend countless
hours whittling away at little poems about existential fatigue that can't
find a good enough reason to rhyme, or listening to Cake's I Will
Survive on repeat. Look! she points out, just a second too late to catch
sight of the flash: all sizzle, ember & arc freshly forking sky. We are
somehow always missing everything, lost inside our own lives or
drowning inside our skin. Look, relax, take a moment to eat
something— something small but nourishing. See this light falling all
around us: the debt to which we owe the muteness of it all. & suddenly
I am thinking of strangers somewhere on the other end of the page
again, as they ask me, a poem, about the plausibility of the future. As I,
the poem, am telling them: *You are it. Don't forget the existence
of joy*

---

* Stop reading this. Throw the book far, far away. Go love somebody now
before it's too late, even if that somebody is You

II

OBJECTS OF OBSCURE POWER

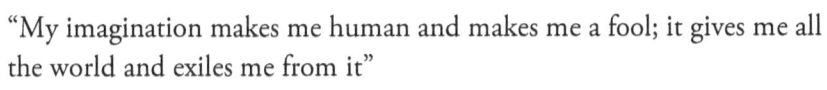

"My imagination makes me human and makes me a fool; it gives me all the world and exiles me from it"

—Ursula K. Le Guin

AUTHOR'S NOTE: Read these pieces in accordance to the prescribed imaginary longitudes + latitudes.

PILLOW FORT

(Otherwise known as an Apocalyptic Fable of Sorts)*

Like every morning before I find myself struggling to patch together a new life somewhere outside of the old, but instead just end up building another pillow fort. Something to hold together until the sheets come crashing down—a modest temple in which to count my mounting loneliness. I find an old broom to hold it all up. Inside angles dream of going not crooked. Pinched-together knots improvise their escape. Milk-colored quilts shudder & ceilings sag like a secondhand circus tent. Rather than leaping light comes clawing its way through ratty zags as silence bends like moonbeam genuflecting in a prism. I sit staring, from morning till midnight, through cracks in the system imagining a somethingness to spare; to gauze over this ink of hollowed nothings & nevermores. Sometimes I might grow a little bored, turn on a fan to replicate a windblown storm or call the dog to come galloping in from another room, catch its fang in a pillowcase just to concoct some minor drama. But on the whole I am steadfast, resolute in the destructions I am willing to pretend into being. All of them pretty in their own way, all of them noble creations. Seahorses swimming in a test tube. With teeth tucked under tongue one might could count them all. *Imagine it:* Everything we've ever built…Every little life we've fated to come crashing down on us & somehow, still, always finding a broom to hold it all up again

---

* Read inside a pillow or blanket fort

PRATTLE OF CHIMES

(Otherwise known as Spit-Soaked Pavane for Broken Wolves[*])

Little furies tumble, sulked from night's blue throat as elder wolves whine on the far edge of town while I putter through these dusty rooms in search of a shuttered window.   *Dear rags of wind:* harvest only half this melancholy; leave the rest for posterity. Every stone sunk at the bottom of the river, all these kites moss-strewn & marooned.   Listen well to the old earth chirruping, having plumbed these pumpernickel years . . . how gently limbs still click outside your door as clockhands devour autumn heart's spindly sigils

---

[*] Read under or near chimes

RAFT

(Otherwise known as Subdued Aria for a Luminescent Nobody[*])

Lilt the stars, fur-backed, silken-peeled from the skies. Life is a most unusual premise: an imperishable pink of aches that fizzles from the rafters. Sing softly in the cadence of rain & chandeliers. Dream a raft of teeth to take you home when the loveless spiders explode. Everything will end as only you intend. Save your rose-hipped self from exsanguination. You are as allowed to fall apart as you are to put yourself back together again

---

[*] Read inside an unfilled bathtub pretending itself to be a spaceship

BROKEN BELL

(Otherwise known as Antibrightbrigade*)

(Here's the thing—I am noticeably absent from my own life.) (

(Sirens bleat; hangnails cut to the quick.))

(((Somehow silence gets stitched into the skin of a bell.)))

((((Loping clouds, *Bemute me*: deliver me unto the swaddling dark.))))(((((

Shove back into Mother Night's pocket all these secondhand stars.)))))

((((((Shutter the stinking violets.))))))

(((((((Only steeples could fathom the cruelty of such brazen brightnesses.
)))))))

(((((((( ))))))))

---

* Read in the woods, sung as one might sing a lullaby to a shadow

OBSCURE GAMES

(Otherwise known as Furniture Islands)*

it is true the boy he did endeavor to dive into Ottomans
collarboneclicking   lungeworthyluscious

Elbowsout, was he but too soon impetuous?
when what little things do dream before their time is due for dreaming he
who, pearl of livingrooms, hippocampused a colander toothplucked the
chandelier

Gone thenafter
the carpet always sprying
how merrily rugburns
do rigamarole!

---

* Read gazing upon the ceiling as if the ceiling is the floor and the floor
the ceiling, or while making snow angels in the carpet

SEAHORSE SCURVY PARADE

(Otherwise known as Junkbutton Heartgalleon[*])

fumblestruck apparatus this loom in
listless idling mode were not we
so delectably chartered? amidst
edgermost maratimes a lonely
anchor squanching along liminal
sharkfodder for infinities buoyed
in
our ambivalence
golumnious the
crustaceans
glyphlets in
alignment
allofthem
offerings
ominous
virulent
rising other
wise
red we wh O
c
ul
d b

---

[*] Read as quickly as humanly possible, tongue-trippingly, while standing on a couch

cr
A
SHI
nG.

HEADLESS DOLL

(Otherwise known as Uncreation Myth*)

In the beginning everything was hate_blighted world twirling on the stitch of a pin_Came chorus of flood: frost upon frost_heatwave upon heatwave_our angel-laden Father God who art garbled in heaven_little quaver of radio waves be Thy Name_His sandlight sieved_trembling through the epochs_thus bespoke Mary Mother_Of Midnight, throat full of scorch_She who, pretend-lit, mythologized a match & coughed up the stars_Next came Story, sputtering forth like first sting of rain_Great wound in the_Sky while all of eternity assiduously twitching_Poetry came later_Clutching its gifts of syllables_Skulls + breath + blood + bones_Blanketed of a flesh so bereft like a_Second skin of longing_Marbled eyes floating up through time's punch bowl_Spiked of dawn's bitter lemons_Pinch of dusk here_Peach pit of melancholy there_& every precious aftermore tumbling toward its hallelujah_Finely gauzed in this_Spindly schism of isms_Tenderest, the gallant most rush of gushingly

---

* Read while clutching a doll or stuffed animal in fatal disrepair

CUCKOO CLOCK

(Otherwise known as One Too Many Day One Too Many One Too Much)*

& one too many suns risen_one too many ways to feel solar eclipsed_one too many heart to lug around like a freak in a jar_this tickled light flooded with formaldehyde_one too many brain sloshing one too many chemicals_much too bubblegum too brazen too bobbleheaded_one too many tattoos much too many sigils to envisage_too angel-beaked too midway not nearly enough Mohawk_one too many doors not nearly enough skeleton keys_one too many myths to swindle not nearly enough saga_ one too many exodus much too many genesis to swish_one too many stars grinning in oblivion much too many skies scalded with coffee rings_ one too many splinters to unprick much too many sawdust to weep_one too many mirrors sawed in half from disgust_one too many loneliness folding over itself like origami longing—you can only fold a sheet so many times_one too much chatter not nearly enough teacups_one too many escalator one too many footfalls to shuffle_one too many painted trees sonorously screaming_one too many mouth much too

many tongues astroturfed_one too many bird bone much too many altars for too small a things to be dead_one too many thimble one too many thumb_one too many head

---

* Read in your favorite hiding place, or facing backwards away from the audience

full of dreaming much too many pillows in which to smuggle this blueblack sorrow_one too many razors never enough sinks but too many tubs to hide the fur_one too many ankle not enough tripwires_one too many books outside I'll never read & inside I'll never write_one too many poem one too many titles_ one too many songs in which to shrink much too many dirges by which to grow tall_one too many breath much too many alkaline to inhale_one too many calendar to multiply much too many remainders_one too many daffodils to snip much too many petals to imperil_one too many words not nearly enough syllables_one too many bells much too many silence_one too many ending much too many infinities_one life too many one life too much still not nearly enough

SKELETON KEY

(Otherwise known as Questions, All of Them Rhetorical[*])

             How   do

    I   even   begin

to   tell   you

       how   all

     the   happy   songs

          hurt

or   the   capacity   of

         rain

    in   even so small an

       amount

       cupped

   in   human hands

  to drown a   face pinched

in   sorrow?

---

[*] Never be read aloud, only written, as small as it can bear to fit in a place that not many people bother to look very often (but there, nonetheless)

SPIRAL STAIRCASE

(Otherwise known as Minor Feral Fragments[*])

bluer skies making ripe for rainbows

sadness unraveling &   all its untold compartments the

many sequestered dreams of a fox   staircase or canyon

gentler rooms in hunt of quieter keys   inverted kingdoms & hidden
symmetries

lurking in this   swish of

thistle-bound under   brush

---

[*] Read near a prismatic rainbow, puddle, or while wearing a hand-made paper mask

III

THREE OMENS

"It is by no means an irrational fancy that, in a future existence, we shall look upon what we think our present existence, as a dream."
— Edgar Allan Poe

AUTHOR'S NOTE: The following pieces are based on dreams I can't remember having yet.

THE PROGNOSTICATORS*

It occurred to all of us about the same time that our little brother could see the truth at the bottom of the well: how all fates entwined, triple-knotted and gleaming in their misery, held together by a wise but stubborn old snake named Mister Misty McRattly Tail, Esquire.

In those days we took turns dangling him by his dusk-colored ankles when we weren't busy picking at scabs on the porch, or catching too-low clouds scudding overhead toward a big pink horizon of demise.

While it was my turn my sister Witch Hazel counted her splinters gleefully while Buck Owen tore apart a rocking chair and Salinger packed an ant pile into an old pie tin. "Look how big the peppercorns panic!" he hooly-hawed, before pouring it down the back of Zipperboy's overalls.

"What's baby see now?" yelled one of em again. I don't know which.

"Getting closer" I reported, lowering the rope cinched round baby's ankles as he giggled furiously into the void. "Good baby. Go go go!"

---

* The following dream also featured a strangely glowing terrarium, but all the fish were missing

The game of it was just so: Noose up thine soft baby ankles and let descend. Get baby close enough to catch snake in mouth. Pull up for a prize. Most days it wasn't about winning—just giving a name to our madness.

Soda bottle chimes clanked together strung from their limbs now. An owl peered out from a knothole. "What's baby see?"

"Not quite yet" I reported, feeling sludgeblooded and starved for action. "First one to brick a bird gets to pet the spider!" one of em announced. I don't know which.

Next thing I know the sky is thick with salmon dust and breathing is a chore. "Cut it" a neighbor hollered. They must had been burning; I could smell it in the air. Disinfected suds and gristle.

Then all were out wide in the yard equidistantly posed: one burning up the kiddy pool, one blowing black bubbles, one pinching mushrooms, one picking for nose coal. Deep diving.

"What's baby see?"

"Almost almost," I reported. Flung my attention down the hole and heard a rising whistle. Like fishhooks swirling around in a bowl made of molars.

Glass clicking through its crooked lips.

Someone yodeled. Another yelled out a word we were taught never to say aloud.

Everyone fell down at once, crashing through the grass itch-riddled and red.

"What's baby see?"

"Nigh coming up" I reported, feeling a sugar high. Sudden summer heat in my bones.

I could feel the future rumbling in my belly, like that pie tin full of ants. Could taste time and rain backwards. Throat full of dandelion parade...little baby bulbs and serpent skulls. Giddy and sad without knowing or caring to know the extent of my own edges.

"What are you children up to now?" said Mother, summoning us for dinner.

Inside, we dunked our heads, said grace, scraped our plates clean.

"So—" Father finally said, slurping his canteen. "How was your day?" In the distance hills were hiccupping; sirens sloshed around like wild bells drunk on panic. Our sheepheads tilted as night was coming on strong, guttering through the slanted board. Mother gnawed a cactus in the disposal.

Everything is wonderful" I said as baby wriggled, laughing through the snake writhing round in its gummy maw. "Why do you ask?"

*ENCORE**

Act I

Here's the thing—the clown isn't laughing. He's just sitting there on his stool in the center of the tent, sharpening his banana into a knife. This is after twisting together a balloon elephant and making my sister cry, popping it with a pin hidden between his teeth.

Just a balloon, Dad said, cracking a peanut. All a part of the show, kiddo. Just watch!

Dad knows best; he wouldn't bring us to something that would disappoint us. Eat some more cotton candy, he says.

I do.

Act II

Who wants to fly? The clown is asking now as trapezists powder their hands. Where's the net?

---

* Ironically, the following dream was tonally rather upbeat, except for the murderous clowns

A few giddy volunteers are hoisted up. They go swinging, slung, caught by their ankles. One slips, doesn't quite make it. A dull thud as lights go out. Clowns dance through the dark smeared in glowing make up, sleepy organ cranking while somebody cleans up the mess with a mop, leaving a puddle of mush in the middle. Weeping mother is ushered backstage by the ringleader. He removes his tall hat out of respect for her sacrifice, all in service of the show. His twisty mustache doesn't flinch.

Now who wants to come down and put their head in the lion's mouth? the clown says.

This time no one is volunteering. Eventually, a father convinces his son to not be chicken. Go on boy, give em a show!

Dads know best; they wouldn't let the lion hurt us.

When the child, hands in pocket, places his head in the lion's mouth he is nervously laughing.

Because what else can you do with your head in a lion's mouth?
Clown with banana knife gives the crowd a wink.

Everyone woos, wahs.

When the big cat's jaw snaps it looks fake. Nameless boy's body with neck nub makes no sound as it falls. Then there are trumpets and tubas and confetti in the air.

What a spectacle eh kiddo? Dad spits out a shell. I honestly don't understand how they did that last trick but everyone is already clapping, so I put my hands together awkwardly. My stomach hurts, tied in triple knots.

Act III

Time for the finale! proclaims the ringleader, back in action. He snaps and they roll out a cannon.

How many kids do you think we can cram inside? he wants to know.

I hold my sister's hand to let her know I'm here. I see it, too.

Other parents are pushing their kids forward now, urging them to climb the ladder and crawl into the cannon's hissing mouth. They do even though it's scary and most of them are crying.

When the man with the tall hat and inflexible mustache lights it a tongue of flame goes licking across the ring, spattering flaps red with specks, black powder residue, and little bits of bone and teeth. Then a spark catches the cloth, goes crawling along the tent's skin.

Dad will know what to do; he wouldn't let any of this happen.

When I turn to him, he's sucking down a peanut. How many people do you know personally who have been murdered by a clown? he puts it to me as I watch people behind him bleeding, stabbed by a murderous clown with a banana knife. They sag, slip down in the cracks like deflated balloons.

Me personally? Well, zero.

There ya go! Dad smiles. Don't be ridiculous.

Act IV

The tent is burning down from the inside. We watch the head clown crawl into his tiny car with ten of his friends and zip away. Its little engine sputters along, tailpipe hiccupping exhaust. A bloody banana peel splashes down in a puddle in front of us, flung out the window.

Before I take my sister out I say goodbye to our parents.

Bye, Dad.

Bye, kiddo.

His eyes are gone. A blankness: glassed-over sheen of swimmy blue. There is nothing there.

Wave goodbye forever, I tell my sister. Her shoulders scrunch.

We watch the tent burning from a safe distance. Smoke curling, poles collapsing. Sky red as a loon's eye. Mom and Dad are sat smiling somewhere still inside. We can hear their hands on fire, clapping through the burning.

Bravo, Bravo!   What a show.

Tomorrow there shall be another.

SECONDHAND HEAVENS*

1.

For years now I have been building a simulator of my life. It's like a cross between *The Sims* & *Minecraft* but only populated with people I like, who like me back, & nothing I'm not already equipped to handle. No monsters, no dungeons, no boss fights. Nothing to fight so no weapons, nor cramped inventories to constantly shuffle around to make room. No health bars or leveling up. No shops, no currency. Just long days glazed with nostalgia & still nights swollen with melancholy. That is, an algorithm of quieter moments, the ones you wish you could've lived inside longer before life snipped them short. Perhaps we're not meant to know what these moments are when they are. Only sense them, like a bruise we know is coming but hasn't yet arrived. Perhaps that unknowing has a purpose to serve? I'm not sure. I'm only 13, & life already feels much longer than I thought it would ever be.

2.

Sometimes a glitch will make it appear as though the earth & sky have switched places, but it's only temporary. Everything snaps back into focus eventually & at night I summon my all old friends into a field. We gather, linger & loiter, strolling through meadows flecked with marigold toward

---

* To this day I still suffer from insomnia. As I child I used to watch the red eye of the smoke alarm battery detector blinking, for hours & hours, until my mind grew weary & I dozed off. This was before I realized I could just tell myself stories instead, which would have the same effect as a smoke alarm battery detector

a fat sun the color of grapefruit. It is more rectangular than it is square. There are mountains too, cascading down the horizon, a few clouds sailing by like wafer-thin rafts. I have programmed the weather here to never rain or snow. I listen to my friends say the same things over & over: a predictable script that will never come as a surprise. One compliments my glasses. Another asks if I'd care to share their chips. A third, whose avatar is not like the others, part of their face missing, wonders aloud how long infinity is. Because my own avatar is mouthless, I do not answer. Instead we wander aimlessly over the hill & down toward the beach, bright coast crackling with static as lidless jellyfish wash onto an edgeless shore. Waiting, waiting—listening to the electric sand hiss.

3.

The day / night cycle here can leave one feeling mildly concussed. Dungeon maps have begun showing up all over my body & I don't know why. I follow them anyway to find the NPC whose face keeps erasing itself, whose ears keep darting off his head – let us call him Omega – in the hall of an empty high school. Lockers bulge, buckle, overflow with sand. Lava oozes out of cracks in the walls like an inscrutable wound as he parrots another line from his slantwise jag of teeth. "You ever get the feeling you did something really bad. Something unforgivable?" I'm too busy watching mushrooms grow in great tufts over a spot where someone has scratched an unspeakable name. I wonder whose locker it could be. "Maybe we get trapped into the thing we loved most? Maybe regret is a loop we live inside forever?" I remain mouthless but meanwhile my mind is racing. I'm thinking of all the ways to conceive of such a place: Labyrinth in search of a minotaur...Snow globe in search of shaking...Spiral in search of unraveling...Reliquary in search of something, anything sacred, to which to cling in an otherwise armless landscape.

4.

If you go far enough, at one corner of the map you'll find a waterfall on fire. At another, a lake featuring enormous hands with every pair of palms open, as if struggling to hold up the sky. Some of the fingers seem awkwardly postured, pinned back implausibly. All the knuckles have rusted. Equidistant apart, no two hands make contact. Looking out over the placid-brackish water, I consider making them touch. Consider how some digits might like to interlock. But as it is, I know I must leave their lattice of longing alone. The map on my skin is twitching, strobing Technicolor like a miniboss on the verge of extinction. I think something might be wrong with paradise.

5.

Desert here is endless. Buzzards wreath a spinnaker sky, shadows swim & quicksand blooms under shuffle-of-feet. Night falls like aching through amber; yells timber. Time, too, has its teeth. Nothing makes sense until it's too late to save but if you prick the moon you can watch it bleed.

6.

There are caves here, too: little subterranean veins washed in lamplight. It's a nice place to get lost & stay lost. Starlight falls through cracks like spiders burning & nothing hurts like it once did. The way life could hurt sometimes, the way loneliness could stretch on forever—fading birds caught in the back of one's throat. Here, in this place of forgetting I tuck my knees, reel back & rock. A blip of lullaby swishes my avatar to sleep. Here, my fake friends won't find me, the ones whose chorus of faces have begun to melt, whose hair have begun to drip off. All of their eyes leak Xs: a cacophonous mob of ominous omission.

7.

There is a bell whose function it is to signal one class passing into the next. In the main office, where a window has been left ajar so callous chatter can filter through the hall, & outlooking a tree whose trunk has been plunged on its nose like a lawn dart, my best friend Omega meets me. By now he is but a pale hologram. Soon he'll be completely erased. A thing I have not programmed is leaping from his mouth again, torn agape by an afternoon breeze carried in from the courtyard: *ANSWER) Limbo: restless state of caught in-betweenness.* I am thinking now of what it means to be in sweet oblivion. Of if, might, was, will never be. The sun tilts, flicked off its axis as bats with bullets for wings scud overhead, their monsoon swarm singing emergency. I trace the map over my skin & know pain is a continent we cannot even begin to touch. "Do you have any queries for me?" Omega is begging. I can't tell if it's because it's his last chance or mine.

8.

I follow my skin map to a place where their destinations converge, the candied bullseye in the center. Next there comes a procession of glitches: coughing up of clocks, sweating of sparrows. Pinpricks of blue needling out of everyone's chests in a virulent rush. All of my friends panic, gridlock of skin marching in lockstep, herding themselves along the precipice of a cliff's lip. They topple one by one like lemmings, yell help before kissing the ground when they are meant to splat, falling through instead. Phantom nets catch the cradles of their bodies, bones gone sludge-soft like porridge.

9.

QUERY) What of the wind that inherits our scars, carries them from one theft-of-night to the next? Of all the secondhand heavens & hand-me-down hells? What of the hollow bells born to never ring, all the trees blooming in reverse, their dark roots exposed to the open air? Broken boughs buried under a terrarium of limestone & beta decay? What of all the remainders of us too frightened too frequent, too many too late to count aloud?

10.

I'd like to tell you what eternity feels like but I can't; it's only something I can hint at, like glimpsing God through a straw. I'd like to tell you what love feels like too. Not the kind they sing about in cheesy pop songs but the kind that goes screaming down your spine when all your numbered days finally run out. The kind of love you cling to, that shatters your bones into a matrix of shame like one last sunset—an unhealable helix of grief, a human heart in the shape of an ellipsis, one that is always inking back like a smudge trying to dream itself whole again. Something that can vanish, which can never be gotten back. Do you understand me? Do you understand now? I'd like to lie & tell you it'll be enough to save you from all the hate of this world. No ruins in the wild that can't be made into a temple. But I can't, because my avatar is mouthless. So instead I'll wander aimlessly over the hill & down toward the beach, bright coast crackling with static as lidless jellyfish wash onto an edgeless shore. Waiting, waiting—listening to this electric sand hiss.

IV

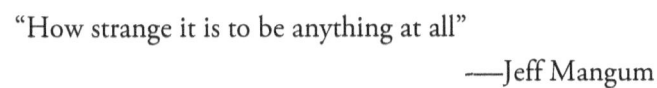

SALUTIS IN SALUTIDINE:

A ROLEPLAYING GAME OF LANGUAGE & LONELINESS

"How strange it is to be anything at all"

——Jeff Mangum

AUTHOR'S NOTE: There is no winning or losing this game, unless you don't play at all.

SALUTIS IN SOLITUDINE

~ a game of language & loneliness ~ Needed: D20 die + paper & pen +
imagination

0. HOW TO "PLAY"

*Every roll is an offering. Take what's given & build a bridge toward
elsewhere. If there's a zipper pinned to a skull projected by a carousel of
camelback riders, open your mouth & accept the gift of a desert.

**In other words, this is a surrealist collaborative game designed to be
played alone. Be a perpetual tourist; write yourself a home within the
holes. You may want to have several sheets of paper ready. Each page
represents a new stage of your journey. You win whenever you reach the
last page. You choose the moment of its arrival.

***Wherever you see a   ⁀,⁀ that is your invitation to react to the
given prompt with your own response.

****Nothing you can do is wrong.

*****Nowhere you can end up is lost.

I. UNPRIMER

STEP ONE: Sit completely still.

STEP TWO: Collect silence.

STEP THREE: Internal playgrounds & powerlines. In-trails not entrails. Float until your throat starts to glow a guttural nonsense song – a larynx ditty of make- believe. When you were but a child every carpet was a castle, every ceiling a sky. It still can be. Trust in Tongue Butterflies. Banish All Magnetism. Let Sleep the Spiders of Cynicism.

STEP FOUR: Beware the Anti-Night Brigade & Hologram Police; Manufactured chrome ghosts of the Cognicoats; Insipid Spindrifts, Sumptuous Ones & Noir-Fanged Fogeaters. {See *Fractious Factions*}.

STEP FIVE: Follow your inner trill to the placeless beyond places: secret chasm between *Inter & Outerspace*

STEP SIX: Seek out inverted skull kingdoms, invest in Surreality Insurance, or witness the Melancholy Parade. It's your trip – every alley of your own design. Circumlocate thy Saturn-Eyes of Inbetween!

STEP SEVEN: Finally, begin to unerase.

STEP EIGHT: Welcome to The Alter.

STEP NINE:

II. THE ALTER

You have arrived at an unreachable place. Here, all windows are walls & strange doors blink with blinding alacrity. You can't tell with any certainty where you're headed, but you know it's a temple. You can hear little machines dancing, chittering sawdust songs full of afterglow. Something like hope awaits you beyond their clockwork calibrations...

Q. What the door is made of:
[roll D20]

1. *Door Made of Rotted Meat* ⚀,⚀ = soft animal it once was?
2. *Door Made of Zippers* ⚀,⚀ = what is keeping it shut?
3. *Door Made of Glinting Knives* ⚀,⚀ = what cannot be cut by it?
4. *Door Made of Jutting Teeth* ⚀,⚀ = what the molars are made of?
5. *Door Made of Swollen Tire Rubber* ⚀,⚀ = their favorite road once driven?
6. *Door Made of Leathery Knotholes* ⚀,⚀ = what imaginary bird lives there?
7. *Door Made of Winking Dolls' Eyes* ⚀,⚀ = the reason they wink so smugly?
8. *Door Made of Licorice* ⚀,⚀ = the secret of its sweetness?
9. *Door Made of Secondhand Combs* ⚀,⚀ = what hair cannot be brushed?
10. Door Made of Pure Void ⚀,⚀ = what created it?
11. *Door Made of Cheese Graters* ⚀,⚀ = what does it smell like?
12. *Door Made of Sifting Quicksand* ⚀,⚀ = what lives swallowed below?
13. Door Made of Razor-Sharp Piano Wire ⚀,⚀ = its favored song?
14. Door Made of Hopelessly Tangled Antlers ⚀,⚀ = what once kind of beast?
15. Door Made of Slithering Mirror ⚀,⚀ = why does it slither so?
16. Door Made of Warped Sunstone ⚀,⚀ = what warped it?

17. Door Made of Impeccably Choreographed Ants ✵=what commands them?

18. Door Made of Melted Birthday Cakes ✵ = a wish never granted?

19. Door Made of Swirling Dust ✵ = what blows it along?

20. *Door Made of Horn & Ivory* ✵ = one illusion? one reality?

Q. What does the One Voice say to you as you pass through the threshold?
[roll D20]

1. "If it can be sold, destroy it: make flame the flint-spit of imagination!"

✵ = what remains priceless?

2. "Only the strange will survive" ✵ = shape of your strangeness?

3. "All will be somber when the hills finally hiccup mountains"

✵ = what is making the shifting landscape so unstable?

4. "In this society we learn to fiercely compete for love & attention. How, with everything reinforcing that system, are we to not equate that love or lapse of love - including our manifold failures to perform for it at every turn - with the love we eventually feel we deserve? How are we to not internalize a vicious economy of self-worth? How do we teach ourselves that we are, each of us, whether the world would have us unlearn it, lovely & lovable creatures deserving of grace, fidelity, forgiveness?"

✵ = a kindness you deserve?

5. "I've lost count of my loneliness" ☄ = an imaginary equation?

6. "Carpe Nihilum."   ☄ = an absence?

7. "Bleed brave birds."   ☄ = an albatross?

8. "We, the motion hungry monsters."
                                           ☄ = an equal but opposite stillness?

9. "Unclasp your mandible to reveal your true mask."
                                           ☄ = an emergent face?

10. "Siphon eternity through this god-straw."
                                           ☄ = something imperceptible?

11. "The cats are always watching."
                                           ☄ = with what color inner eyes?

12. [pterodactyl screeching]   ☄ = [a reptilian texture?]

13. "What if the waterfalls are chasing you?"   ☄ = chase them back?

14. "The world needs a fool tilting at windmills."
          ☄ = why is a tooth to be prized much more than a diamond?

15. "Take nothing for granite."
          ☄ = what hastens amber more than age's glaring amulet?

16. "Patient as the pendulum swings."

$\ddot{\smile},\ddot{\smile}$ = shuffling toward eternity how?

17. "Infinite, inviolable mischief." $\ddot{\smile},\ddot{\smile}$ = what infinity feels like?

18. "01100010 01101100 01101001 01101110 01101011 00100000
01101111 01101110 01100011 01100101 00100000 01101001
01100110 00100000 01111001 01101111 01110101 00100000
01110101 01101110 01100100 01100101 01110010 01110011
01110100 01100001 01101110 01100100 00100000 01101101
01100001 01100011 01101000 01101001 01101110 01100101
00101110"

$\ddot{\smile},\ddot{\smile}$ = huh?

19. "The hour of sheep counting people approacheth!"

$\ddot{\smile},\ddot{\smile}$ = a tender wolf? a cruel clock?

20. "The sky is a liar." $\ddot{\smile},\ddot{\smile}$ = night's porous truth?

III. CHARACTER CREATION

~Create Your Own from Scratch: A Questionnaire~

A Sigil or Symbol by Which You Were Once Known:

A Sigil or Symbol Toward Your Becoming:

A Sigil or Symbol That Remains Unknowable:

An Imaginary Landscape You Are Prone to Visiting in Dreams: EX:
Inverted Forest, Poppy Field (Wizard of Oz), Half-Melted Diner

Object of Obscure Power: ⛬ = totem to which you've always been drawn, which in The Alter may grant you great powers, possibly transformed into a weapon?
EX: Rubik's Cube, Spiral Staircase, Headless Doll

Favorite Childhood Game: ⛬ = include any house rules you observed
EX: Floor is Lava, Ghost in the Graveyard (Hide n' Seek at night), Hopscotch

---

Number & Corresponding Personality: ⛬ = soon to be your guide in The Alter/ first words it utters to welcome you
EX: 7- a tall lukewarm stranger, 303- misfit with wrists like rain, 0- cat-faced clown

---

Irrational Enemy: ⛬ = a particularly scabrous malady
EX: Uncanny Valley Effect, Umbrellas, Balloon Full of Scalding Coffee

---

Favorite Song Played Backwards: ⛬ = portion of lyrics written backwards NOTE: If song already backwards, song now appears forwards
EX: Any Nocturne by Chopin, Video Game Theme, Revolution 9 by The Beatles

---

Book You Would Be Reborn As : ⛧,⛧ = designate binding & spine construction

EX: Theoretical Physics Textbook, Nintendo Power, A Midwinter Day's Nightmare

---

Myth or Fable That Doesn't Exist: ⛧,⛧ = a trial that must be undertaken, transfiguration, curse that must be lifted, or magical boon?

EX: Clock Made of Carrot Milk, Thief in the Undertow, Negative Midnight Man

---

IV. BESTIARY

Uncommon Fiends or Faux Friendly Foes:
{for all below ⌖ = description? + special attack? + where it lives?} [roll D20]

1. Murderous Shadow Puppets ⌖ =
2. Animated Cutlery ⌖ =
3. Sentient Sharp Paper ⌖ =
4. Vox Zombies ⌖ =
5. Little Good Wolf ⌖ =
6. Silence ⌖ =
7. Chandelier Made of Teeth ⌖ =
8. Peter Pan's Stitched-On Shadow ⌖ =
9. Exploding Sparrow ⌖ =
10. Rain of Truth ⌖ =
11. Extraterrestrial Glyph ⌖ =
12. Leering Painting ⌖ =
13. Bored Minotaur ⌖ =
14. Fatal Lullaby ⌖ =
15. Gelatinous Bear ⌖ =
16. Floating Guillotine ⌖ =
17. Petulant Cube ⌖ =
18. Carnivorous Mirror ⌖ =
19. Razorwind ⌖ =
20. Book Full of Endings ⌖ =

Fractious Factions:

{for all below ☼ = outward appearance? + what they really are? + agenda?} [roll D20]

1. Anti-Night Brigade ☼ =
2. Hologram Police ☼ =
3. Cognicoats ☼ =
4. Insipid Spindrifts ☼ =
5. Sumptuous Ones ☼ =
6. Noir-Fanged Fogeaters ☼ =
7. Deep Marrowed ☼ =
8. Human Zoo ☼ =
9. Antimatter ☼ =
10. Quantum Gargoyles ☼ =
11. Nameless Infinite ☼ =
12. Unshadow ☼ =
13. Spectral Gizzards ☼ =
14. Haunter in the Dark ☼ =
15. Polarity Force ☼ =
16. Queen of Papercuts ☼ =
17. Thistlethorn Fairy ☼ =
18. The Numinous ☼ =
19. Insomniac Machine ☼ =
20. Gadzook, Gladboy, & Olly Olly Oxen Free ☼ =

V. ASSORTED TABLES

Favorite Line(s) from a Kenneth Patchen Poem:

{for all below ✲ = to each line reply with an unrequited epistle} [roll D20]

1. "Who made the snow waits where love is" ✲ =

2. "As we are so wonderfully done with each other / We can walk into our separate sleep / On floors of music where the milkwhite cloak of childhood lies" ✲ =

3. "Be music, night" ✲ =

4. "Any person who loves another person, / Wherever in the world, is with us in this room - / Even though there are battlefields" ✲ =

5. "And light was everywhere and a soft voice saying / You can stop crying now. / (what can we talk about that will take all night? / and I said that I didn't know.) / You can stop crying now" ✲ =

6. "Ghosts in packs like dogs grinning at ghosts" ✲ =

7. "All your damn horses climbing to heaven" ✲ =

8. "The Orange bears with soft friendly eyes / Who played with me when I was ten" ✲ =

9. "Art is not to throw light but to be light..." ✲ =

10. "This is the evening of the two-fisted prayer" ✲ =

11. "Nobody's a long time" ✲ =

12. "To forgive the beautiful its disconsolate deceit / To flash his vengeful badge at every abyss / To HAPPEN / It is the artist's duty to be alive" ✲ =

13. "Now is the time to believe / When there is nothing to believe in!" ✲ =

14. "Have you wondered why all the windows / in heaven were / broken?" ✲ =

15. "We looked to find / An open door, an utter deed of love"
☼ =

16. "Everywhere is a tent where we put on our whirling show"
☼ =

17. "Eyes peer out of the seaweed that gently sways / Above the towers and salt gates of a lost world" ☼ =

18. "Dear reader, gentle reader, dainty little reader, this is / the way we go round the milktrucks and seamusic" ☼ =

19. "But the snake strikes, in a velvet arc / Of murderous speed — assassin beautiful" ☼ =

20. "Who are the people of this unscaled heaven?" ☼ =

Your Safe Place:
{for all below ☼ = a solace that makes it so?} [roll D20]

1. A pillow fort ☼ =

2. Inside the sheets of your bed; as long you keep them tucked tight nothing can touch you ☼ =

3. Labyrinth of a prism's manifold dimensions ☼ =

4. Within the gentle folds of a lilting lullaby ☼ =

5. Under the crook of a swaying slide ☼ =

6. Hushed-away silence inside a keyhole ☼ =

7. Weeping Oubliette ☼ =

8. Curve of a spoon ☼ =

9. Fjord of a fork ☼ =

10. Bivouac of a butter knife ☼ =

11. Nested in the spiral of a nautilus shell ☼ =

12. On the wing of a slaked sky ☼ =

13. Swish of an Octopus' Eyelid ☼ =

14. Sumptuous tundra ☼,☼ =

15. Listening to rain click under a mushroom cap ☼,☼ =

16. Inverted Playground ☼,☼ =

17. Far End of a Rabbithole ☼,☼ =

18. Dollhouse roughly the size of a regular-sized house ☼,☼ =

19. In the bough of an ancient tree ☼,☼ =

20. Twisting iris of an oblique hourglass ☼,☼ =

Musical Instrument:

{for all below ☼,☼ = description of its sound? + name of an imaginary song?} [roll D20]

1. A Fleet of Theremins ☼,☼ =

2. A Palimpsest of Piccolos ☼,☼ =

3. A Violence of Violins ☼,☼ =

4. A Feral of Fire Organs ☼,☼ =

5. A Synchronicity of Sharpsichords ☼,☼ =

6. A Belligerence of Luscious Laserbasses ☼,☼ =

7. A Fulcrum of Flubas ☼,☼ =

8. A Callousness of Contrabass Balalaikas ☼,☼ =

9. An Irritant of Friction Harps ☼,☼ =

10. A Bevy of Melodramatic Moogs ☼,☼ =

11. A Heartbreaking Tuning Fork of Staggering Genius ☼,☼ =

12. A Diadem of Didgeridoos ☼,☼ =

13. A Harem of Hurdy-Gurdys ☼,☼ =

14. An Irksome of Otamatones ☼,☼ =

15. A Piquancy of Pikasso Guitars ☼,☼ =

16. An Ouroboros of Aeoluses ☼,☼ =

17. A Shirking Flux of Fifes ☼,☼ =

18. An Admonition of Aztec Death Whistles =

19. A Bathtub Full of Bagpipes =

20. A Shit Ton of Shrieking Keytars =

Nonsense Incantations Which When Uttered Unlock a Temporal Disjunction:
{for all below , = catastrophic details of subsequent temporal disjunction?} [roll D20]

1. Parallax Anomaly =
2. Iota Olio =
3. Ocelot Anemone =
4. Mollycoddle Caterwaul =
5. Apoplectic Requiem =
6. Feckless Kerfuffle =
7. Cockamamie Hullabaloo =
8. Effervescent Buffoon =
9. Byzantine Smithereens =
10. Skedaddle Penumbra =
11. Incognito Shindig =
12. Scintilla Asunder =
13. Hirsute Flautists =
14. Persnickety Derelicts =
15. Scree Smitten =
16. Serendipity Doodah =
17. Jugular Skullduggery =
18. Amoeba Run Amok =
19. Luscious Linoleum =
20. Succulent Shoegaze =

Further Nonsense Incantations Which When Uttered Unlock a Temporal Disjunction:

{for all below ☼ = catastrophic details of subsequent temporal disjunction?} [roll D20]

1. Claptrap Hobbyhorse ☼ =
2. Aurora Borealis Bustier ☼ =
3. Flummox Elixir ☼ =
4. Entropic Lozenge ☼ =
5. Galosh Fiasco ☼ =
6. Bungalow Brouhaha ☼ =
7. Serpentine Silhouette ☼ =
8. Voluptuous Palimpsest ☼ =
9. Episcopalian Ukulele ☼ =
10. Manifest Sonata ☼ =
11. Gossamer Tsunami ☼ =
12. Spindrift Mendicants ☼ =
13. Mellifluous Meander ☼ =
14. Chartreuse Tantrum ☼ =
15. Shenanigan Lagoon ☼ =
16. Gazebo Dragoon ☼ =
17. Paradigm Death ☼ =
18. Apparatus Override ☼ =
19. Apocryphal Ficus ☼ =
20. Diarrhea Ennui ☼ =

Something Is Happening!

[roll D20]

1. You crawl into a giant vacant turtle shell which begins to shuffle forward. Two words: TURTLE TANK.

   ⁍ = the enemy fast approaching?

2. A war is raging! Upon closer inspection the battlefield appears to be occupied by two opposing armies made up of past versions of yourself versus future versions of yourself.

   ⁍ = how the war will end?

3. You fall asleep wearing headphones & wake up to find yourself lost in a tangled jungle of overgrown wires. Hurry up & imagine a machete.

   ⁍ = the last song you heard that made a jungle appear?

4. Reading your favorite book under a tree, you are zapped by lightning. Soon you find yourself trapped inside its pages, but something is different: the hero is now the villain, the villain the hero?

   ⁍ = the book? + heroic villain? + villainous hero?

5. Diabolical bubbles!

   ⁍ = why have they come for you?

6. You begin to unspool a thread from your shirt which grows thicker, heavier on the floor until the coil of fabric is writhing underfoot.

   ⁍ = the garment snake's secret?

7. A certain window in the apartment reveals 5 minutes into the future. You become addicted to sitting there watching pedestrians pass by. You will never know those looking in are seeing 5 years into the past.

   ⁍ = what do they see looking in?

8. It's raining pickles.

⛬ = what your umbrella is made of?

9. You awake on a pixelated island. The sky is cantaloupe. Every flower sways to a symphony of blips.

⛬ = your avatar's form? + the point of this game?

10. An algorithm has glitched somewhere. Everywhere you look escalators scrawl the sky like roving robotic elbows.

⛬ = how we will fix what's broken?

11. Colors in dreams you've never known before. Textures you've never felt. Impossible shapes: edgeless & unfathomable. \

⛬ = a litany of possibilities?

12. There's an alligator in your living room smoking a pipe.

⛬ = his appointment's purpose?

13. Someone sits inventing a calculator of forgiveness by a well.

⛬ = an obsolete abacus of regret?

14. An ocean bulging with bathtub pirate ships. Buoyant the clawfoot galleons bob as mermaids glitter through froth-frosted waves.

⛬ = in search of what twilit treasure?

15. You have arrived at the center of the Earth: your childhood bedroom.

⛬ = what the wall wears?

16. Gravity has reversed. Trees rocket out of the landscape, sucked into the All-Consuming Zenith- Eye. Good thing you have invented something for this fated date of doom.

⛬ = a prophetic invention?

17. The Catalog of Wishful Forbidden Contraband arrives in your mailbox. You can't quite make out the company of origin. {50% chance of *Charmed Slightly Alluring Loot*, 50% chance of *Cursed Slightly Disconcerting Loot*}

☽,☆ = something not easily consumable?

18. Exploring the ruins of The Vex, you are assailed by a bouncing troop of spherical chirping automatons.

☽,☆ = an intrepid chase sequence?

19. Nobody in this movie theater seems to believe you when you tell them the movie currently playing is exactly your life, in exactly the way it all happened. Slurping of soda, smacking of popcorn grows louder.

☽,☆ = the trailer before the movie?

20. You are caught in the tunnel between a wizard & a samurai. A timeless showdown is about to ensue!

☽,☆ = an ancient grudge?

Lost in the Never-Ending Strip Mall:

{for all below ☽,☆ = what happens next?} [roll D20]

1.   Flooded floor. Lone employee in a boat says he's been searching for an exit for a week.   ☽,☆ =

2.   Luggage carousel lurches. Lone bag is worth 3 rolls of *Cursed Slightly Disconcerting Loot.*   ☽,☆ =

3.   Floor gets thinner & thinner until player can't fit through .
☽,☆ =

4.   Writers' conference. Some charge at each other with their CVs stapled to their foreheads. Others cloak themselves delicately in suits of origami armor. Words wince, flicker, flash everywhere. One announces he is the king of all poetry. He is soon challenged to a duel by the self-proclaimed queen of all prose. They both drink ink until they explode.   ☽,☆ =

5.   Warehouse of guns that fire only nice things: kites, kittens, flowers.
☽,☆ =

6. Floor full of doorknobs. 🎲 =

7. Empty library. All books have blank pages. Low drums can be heard in the distance. 🎲 =

8. Artificial jungle. Encounter psionic fruit. 🎲 =

9. Aisles & aisles of phone booths. Every line, the same voice keeps calling. 🎲 =

10. Casino. All the slots jackpot until winning is meaningless. 🎲 =

11. Factory full of other, smaller factories. They all make nesting dolls. 🎲 =

12. Room full of pink electric fog. 🎲 =

13. Mindgnawer nest! So musty. RUN! 🎲 =

14. Dogs playing poker 🎲 =

15. Random objects afloat in midair. One impossibly long equation is written on the wall. 🎲 =

16. Tiny room. The Slothman challenges you to a fatal game of *rock, paper, scissors*. 🎲 =

17. Ocean of giant stuffed dolls. A giant claw. You are the prize! 🎲 =

18. Mountain of junk. May scavenge for random items here. Small chance of getting pricked with something sharp, which prompts a psionic reaction. 🎲 =

19. Floor of no consequence. Few faceless people meandering. 🎲 =

20. A mystical vending machine contains 1 *Charmed Slightly Alluring Loot*. 🎲 =

Charmed Slightly Alluring Loot:
{for all below: ,: = one-sentence descriptor? + object's effect?} [roll D20]

1. ANTIMATTER WHIP :,: =
2. MIRRORED TRENCH :,: =
3. MORROW MASK :,: =
4. SURREALITY PISTOL :,: =
5. PROMETHEAN FLAME :,: =
6. EFFERVESCENT FIST :,: =
7. ENCASED VOID :,: =
8. FRACTAL SHOTGUN :,: =
9. HORN OF BLACK UNICORN :,: =
10. BOOK OF HATE :,: =
11. VOX REPEATER :,: =
12. ANTIMATTER BOW :,: =
13. ASTRAL TEMPEST :,: =
14. PRANCING POCKET PONY :,: =
15. GHOST REVOLVER :,: =
16. ANTIMATTER BLADE :,: =
17. COMPASS TOWARD TRUE SELF :,: =
18. QUANTUM HARP :,: =
19. ANTIMATTER DAGGER :,: =
20. SUN IN A BOTTLE :,: =

Cursed Slightly Disconcerting Loot:
{for all below: ,: = one-sentence descriptor? + object's effect?} [roll D20]

1. ASTRAL DUMMY :,: =

2. MOON TRAPPED IN A THIMBLE　　☼ =
3. SATURN SCYTHE ☼ =
4. VORPAL TENT ☼ =
5. ATOMIZER ☼ =
6. SECOND SKIN ☼ =
7. NUCLEAR FEATHER ☼ =
8. SINGLE SHARD OF ANTIMATTER ☼ =
9. WORMHOLE IN A LUNCHBOX ☼ =
10. TECHNICOLOR NOOSE ☼ =
11. FRACTAL GRENADE ☼ =
12. DARK FIBERS BOW ☼ =
13. TELEKINETIC TRIPWIRE ☼ =
14. BANANA KNIFE ☼ =
15. TIME HULA HOOP ☼ =
16. LUCKY HUMAN'S FOOT ☼ =
17. JUST A REGULAR OLD RADISH ☼ =
18. PROCRUSTEAN BED ☼ =
19. CONTAGIOUS YAWN ☼ =
20. RAVENOUS PRISM ☼ =

The End? {when you arrive at the last page – again, you choose the time of your arrival - this is what happens . . .}
[roll D20]

1. Coughing up a mouthful of skeleton keys in the garden, you tilt your head back at the Red House.　☼ = what will bloom now?
2. You arrive, finally, at the Carnival of Inanities. All is a splendor of tedium. You are grateful for every little insignificant moment. ☼ = a kind of carousel?

3. Every flower that was once a scab. ∵,∵ = the bees that feed?

4. A horned monster gnaws at the air in the alley. You could run. You should run. Right? ∵,∵ = how it was wounded?

5. An electric orchard. Seahorses sizzle in every filament. ∵,∵ = neon juices?

6. Somewhere along the way you became obsessed with speed playthroughs. Every game, every challenge, every glitch greeted with uncannily fast reflexes under breakneck conditions. But you couldn't stop. One day your own life began to hurry too, galloping along at such a rate you couldn't fling a blink behind you to feast upon the graphics of the moment—to eat the spectacle or drink in details. Now goodbyes blear by like rain wincing on a windshield. It's not too late to slow the procession of the Melancholy Parade. ∵,∵ = something to shrink time?

7. The Museum of You is now officially open . ∵,∵ = exhibits?

8. Little storms that need no name. ∵,∵ = your inner weather?

9. Creatures made of glass surround you. ∵,∵ = are they singing or screaming?

10. "This time, let's try following the red brick road instead shall we?" says the dithering man full of straw. ∵,∵ = what wonderous worlds await?

11. With a pocket full of glittering tokens, you stroll into the Arcade of Omniternal Siliance. ∵,∵ = featured games?

12. It is your first day at the School of Unlearning ∵,∵ = your classes?

13. A flying birdhouse has carried you far, far away ∵,∵ = what wings will rise?

14. An amusement park for ghosts . ∵,∵ = a few attractions?

15. In this place that's always midnight, rock & roll legends congregate, jam together sipping shots of quicksilver nostalgia. ∵,∵ = some anachronistic collaborations?

16. A soapskin palace has been hollowed through here with invisible

worms. Its sweet- smelling rind bubbles beneath a basin sun.

☼ = what won't melt it?

17. When co-existing with this reality became a chore, you decided to carve a new one out of secondhand hope. ☼ = what crystals may be plucked through tearducts?

18. A village built out of silverware quakes as clouds of sausage rain down in droves. Zagtooth mouths of gutters elongate.

☼ = saddest flavor ice cream?

19. There are no shortcuts to reach the places that matter most. ☼ = solemn but singsong beginning?

20. Whoever you are right now is enough.   ☼ = a truth that has always remained true?

ABOUT THE AUTHOR

Matthew Burnside's forthcoming books include *Centrifugal: Unstories* (Whiskey Tit) and *Skull Kingdoms: An Imaginary Omnibus* (Unsolicited Press). He is the author of *Wiki of Infinite Sorrows* and *Postludes* (both from KERNPUNKT), *Rules to Win the Game* (Spuyten Duyvil Press), *Dear Wolfmother* (Heavy Feather Review), and *Meditations of the Nameless Infinite* (Robocup Press). He lives in Virginia and teaches at Hollins University."

ABOUT THE PRESS

Unsolicited Press is based out of Portland, Oregon and focuses on the works of the unsung and underrepresented. As a womxn-owned, all-volunteer small publisher that doesn't worry about profits as much as championing exceptional literature, we have the privilege of partnering with authors skirting the fringes of the lit world. We've worked with emerging and award-winning authors such as Tara Stillions Whitehead, Heather Lang Cassera, Shann Ray, Amy Shimshon-Santo, Brook Bhagat, Kris Amos, and John W. Bateman.

Learn more at unsolicitedpress.com. Find us on twitter and instagram.

www.ingramcontent.com/pod-product-compliance
Lightning Source LLC
Chambersburg PA
CBHW031250120626
46545CB00007B/2734